DON'T TELL ME THAT!

*For the Faculty of the
Lutherischen Theologischen Hochschule
Oberursel, Germany*

Don't Tell Me That!

FROM MARTIN LUTHER'S *ANTINOMIAN THESES*

Translated and Adapted by
Paul Strawn

Lutheran Press
Minneapolis

Lutheran Press, Minneapolis 55449
© 2004 by Lutheran Press
All rights reserved.
Printed in the United States of America.

ISBN 0-9748529-2-9

Library of Congress Control Number: 2004109328

Scripture quotations marked (ESV) are from The Holy Bible, English Standard Version, copyright © 2001 by Crossway Bibles, a division of Good News Publishers. Used by permission. All rights reserved. Capitalization of pronouns referring to the Trinity has been added and is not part of the original English Standard Version text.

Swan logo is a LifeART image © 2004 Lippincott Williams & Wilkins. All rights reserved.

Book design by Scott Krieger.
Cover art and design by Joseph Baumgarn.

TABLE OF CONTENTS

	FOREWORD	7
1	WHAT IS REPENTANCE?	19
2	DO CHRISTIANS REALLY NEED THE LAW?	23
3	NOT TO MAKE US RIGHT BEFORE GOD!	27
4	BUT TO EXPOSE SIN, WRATH AND DEATH	31
5	CHRISTIAN REPENTANCE IS CONTINUAL	37
6	THE LORD'S PRAYER IS A PRAYER OF REPENTANCE	41
7	THE FORGIVENESS OF SIN IS CERTAIN	45
8	REPENTANCE, HOWEVER, IS VITAL!	49
9	THE LAW RULES OVER MAN AS LONG AS HE LIVES	55
10	THE LAW RULES OVER NON-CHRISTIANS AS WELL	59
11	IN CHRISTIANS THE LAW REMAINS UNFULFILLED	63
12	THE LAW MUST CONDEMN	67
	AFTERWORD	71
	BIBLICAL REFERENCES	77

Foreword

"Don't tell me that!"

−*A Small Strawn Child*

I do not remember which one of our children spoke the words above. It was probably one of the boys.

I do not remember the situation exactly. Let's just say, a particular boy, probably around the age of three at the time, had purposely broken one of his toys, and then hidden it under his bed.

I do remember finding something destroyed that should not have been, and asking him if knew anything about its mangled state. From the look on his face, I knew he did. I also knew he had done the mangling!

Just to be sure, however, I stated simply and clearly: "You broke the toy." That did it.

Tears flowed. His hands went up to ears. His mouth opened and out came the words I have never forgotten: "DON'T TELL ME THAT!"

This was fascinating. Viewing the mangled toy had troubled him. But what really hurt was having to hear with his own ears that he was the one who had mangled the toy! His three-year-old solution? Cover his ears!

Why the difference between seeing and hearing? Why the revulsion at hearing stated what he had, in fact, done? What had happened? The Law of God had done its work. Yes, even upon one so small! "*Yet if it had not been for the law,*" the Apostle Paul wrote in his Epistle to the Romans, "*I would not have known sin. I would not have known what it is to covet if the law had not said, "You shall not covet." But sin seizing an opportunity through the commandment, produced in me all kinds of covetousness. Apart from the law, sin lies dead*" (7:7-8).

According to Jesus Christ, this exposing of sin by the Law is actually a work of the Holy Spirit. "*And when He comes,*" Jesus told His disciples concerning the Holy Spirit, "*He will convict the world concerning sin and righteousness and judgment*" (John 16:8).

What this means is that just by stating what was true, that my son had done something he should not have done (in this case, broken the Seventh Commandment by not maintaining and preserving that which was entrusted to him), the Holy Spirit convicted Him of his sin as surely as the words of the prophet Nathan convicted David of his sins with Bathsheba (2 Samuel 12:7). Being so confronted, David repented, and repented heartily.

Without such a confrontation, David's sins would have remained dead.

That is, David's adultery with Bathsheba, and his murder of her husband Uriah, would not have caused David to repent. In fact, without Nathan stating the obvious, David would have kept on living his life–probably in much the same way as my son would have continued to live his life with that mangled toy safely hidden underneath his bed!

Reflecting upon my son's reaction to the declaration of his role in its destruction, I realize that his reaction to the Law of God is not unique. In fact, it just may be that the Church at large itself is currently in the process of lifting up its hands collectively to stop its ears and scream out to its pastors, priests, ministers, professors, teachers, worship leaders and authors: "DON'T TELL ME THAT!"

What do I mean? Well, it could just be that there is a general uprising in the Church nowadays against any preaching, teaching, ministering and music which would involve the Holy Spirit, through the Word of God, convicting hearts of sin (cf. Romans 3:20), and consequently, causing guilt. Now I may be wrong here, but what modern Christian ears seem to want to hear, what Christian minds want to contemplate, what Christian emotions want to feel is not guilt, but joy!

But what Christian could be against such a longing? After all, joy is a *fruit of the Spirit* as noted by the Apostle Paul in his letter to the Galatians (5:22-23)! Certainly if given the choice between guilt and joy, it would be a no-brainer: Joy would win out every time!

Come to think of it, even the great Reformer Martin Luther (1483-1546) was pro-joy! Writing in his *Commentary on the Book of Jonah* back in 1525, for example, Luther noted that our heavenly Father wants us to be joyful:

"...We should learn that God does not want people to be sad and that He hates sad thoughts and sayings, and doctrines which oppress us. He makes our hearts joyful. For He did not send His Son to make us sad, but to make us glad. That is why the prophets and apostles and the Lord Christ Himself admonishes us and even commands us at all times to be joyful and of good cheer (as in Zechariah 9:9), 'Rejoice greatly, O daughter of Zion; shout, O daughter of Jerusalem', and many times in the Psalms, 'Let us rejoice in the Lord', and St. Paul in Philippians (4:4), 'Rejoice in the Lord always'; and Christ (Luke 10:20), 'Rejoice because your names are written in heaven'. Where there is this joy of the Spirit there is a dear joy in the heart through faith in Christ, and we know of a certainty that He is our Savior and High Priest, and this joy is seen in the things we say and do."[1]

But is the joy about which Luther writes here just *any* joy? Is the joy about which Paul writes in Galatians simply a surging emotion of expectancy and contentment —no matter what its cause or reason? More to the point: Is the joy which is a gift of the Holy Spirit the result of simply overlooking, denying, or ignoring sin? That is, of shoving sin under our beds, so to speak, and forgetting about it?

To go at this question in another way: Should I have, upon finding the mangled toy, simply ignored it and rejoiced that my son had so much energy? Should my son have, upon hearing that he had broken his toy, simply ignored the fact that he had done it, and rejoiced? Should David have, upon hearing that he had committed adultery with Bathsheba and then murdered her husband Uriah, simply rejoiced?

If not, why? Well, the joy of which Paul writes in Galatians and upon which Luther expounds in his *Jonah Commentary* is a bit more complex than that. The joy of the Christian is not simply some common type of joy like that experienced when we witness a home run in the bottom of the ninth, participate in a Super Bowl victory parade, or receive a promotion at work. It is a joy that flows from the relief of guilt experienced by my son, by David, and a whole host of Christians through the ages. It is the joy that can only follow the confession of sin and the conviction, by means of the Holy Spirit working through the Word of God, that sin has been forgiven because of the atonement of Christ on the cross for that sin.

So David, after being confronted by Nathan, does not speak of simple joy, of common joy, but of the joy of salvation being returned to him in the firm confidence that his sins had been forgiven:

"Create in me a clean heart O God and renew a right spirit within me. Cast me not away from your presence, and take not your Holy Spirit from me. Restore to me the joy of your salvation and uphold me with a willing spirit" (Psalm 51:10-12).

So if Christian joy is tied so closely to guilt, why the running away from guilt? Has the Church simply come to the point of wanting to skip the 'guilt' part of life and go right to the joy? Has the Church discovered that it is easier, more peaceful, and more appealing, to shun guilt and promote joy?

At this point you may be thinking: "Well, is that not what the Christian Church–of all institutions in society–should do? Should not the Church promote joy? Should not the Church simply welcome, with open arms, anyone and everyone, regardless of how they live? After all, did not Jesus eat with tax collectors and prostitutes? Who are WE then to condemn anyone? Who are WE to make anyone feel guilt in any way shape or form? Should not the Christian life be a life of joy, a joy based upon not having to worry about who we are, and what we are doing?

The only problem with this line of thinking, of course, is that Jesus Christ Himself, the 'founder' of Christianity, frequently spoke about guilt. In fact, Jesus' first public sermon, according to the Gospel of Mark, was this: "The time is fulfilled, and the Kingdom of God is at hand; repent and believe in the gospel."[2]

No one repents unless he is actually guilty of committing a sin, hears that he is guilty, and in admitting that he has committed the sin mentioned, feels that he is guilty. In other words, for someone to repent he must first admit that there is something for which he needs to repent! For someone to repent, he must first feel the guilt of sin.

Granted, the usage of guilt within the Christian Church has gotten out of hand in the past. For hundreds of years, for example, Christians all over the world lived lives of guilt—a guilt that led to a fear of death.

Christians lived in fear of death for they were taught that upon dying, chances were, that they would not go to heaven. Instead, they would end up in purgatory.

Now purgatory was not hell. It was, instead, a place where Christians would be given as much time as they needed to make up for the sins that they committed on earth, but hadn't had the chance to make up for on earth before they died. In other words, *purgatory* was a place where Christians would be *purged* of sin and guilt.

Sure, it was somewhat comforting to think that upon dying, a person would not be sent to hell, but to this purgatory place. Yet, purgatory itself intimidated. Why? Popular wisdom taught that it could take hundreds of thousands of years in purgatory to make up for the sins committed during a few decades of life on earth.

What was even worse was that Christian guilt became a money-making tool for the Church. What better way to generate funds than to promise a reduction of time spent in purgatory if something was done by the Christian while living that would benefit the Church (participation in a crusade, a pilgrimage, a cash donation)?

Enter the obscure German monk, Martin Luther, mentioned above, who in the first of *95 Theses* which he posted in Wittenberg at the end of October, 1517, for academic discussion, began what has since been known as the Reformation of the Church. This is relatively well known.

What is not as well known is that the Reformation of

the Church began with a discussion of guilt and repentance. The very first of the *95 Theses* approached the subject head on, asserting that the Church needed to think about repentance, needed to think about guilt, in a different way than it was at the time: "When our Lord and Master, Jesus Christ, said 'Repent,' he meant that the *whole life* of the believers should be one of repentance."

Now what does that mean? How can the entire life of the Christian be one of repentance? Does that not mean that the entire life of the Christian should be one of guilt?

No, it does not. It does mean, however, that the Christian life should be *real*.

What do I mean? I mean that the Christian, of all people, should realize that since he is still confronted by death, he is still confronted by sin—the ultimate cause of death! Being confronted by sin, the Christian himself should not shy away from its existence, but admit, that yes, sin does exist and he, the Christian, is sinful. Repentance is therefore not a once-in-awhile type of situation, but a Christian's state of being.

Yes, a Christian, through faith in Jesus Christ, has been redeemed by Christ and is now considered to be justified before the Father in Heaven. The Christian, through the Word of God and the Sacraments, has received and continues to receive the Holy Spirit, and the Holy Spirit works within the Christian to produce His fruits, one of which is joy. The Christian's sin, however, remains. It remains to bother, to haunt, to trouble, to perturb, and ultimately to kill.

There is a tension then in Christian joy. A tension caused by the fact that the Christian is redeemed from sin, but remains in sin. A tension which has been captured by the pericopes read on "Joy Sunday" (Jubilate Sunday) within the Church for over 1000 years! On the third Sunday after Easter, texts are read from Lamentations (3:22-33), 1 John (3:1-3), and the Gospel of John (16:16-22) all of which point to the fact that the final and complete rejoicing of the Christian will be when Christ returns again in glory. Until that time, a Christian's rejoicing, a Christian's joy, is always tempered by the ongoing reality of sin.

As long as the Christian realizes this, spiritually he is in a 'good place', as people say. In fact, he is very much like the Apostle Paul describes himself in Romans 7.

When a Christian ignores, or would run away from, the fact that sin is still a daily part of his life, trouble begins. He begins to ignore the sin that still plagues him, or even worse, begins to believe that his heavenly Father loves him for the good things he does.

Unfortunately, the Christian Church nowadays, in its attempt to appeal to the masses, seems to be encouraging, perhaps unwittingly, this type of Christian life. It is doing this by re-imaging itself, by making itself a guilt-free, non shame-based zone. The Church is doing such a thing by seeking to establish itself solely as a place of joy.

To accomplish this make-over, however, certain aspects of Christian life are in the process of being jettisoned. Sermons which would seek to establish the guilt of sin within the Christian (or even simply mention it) have had to go. Hymns and songs which speak of such guilt have had to go. Music which would promote the contemplation of guilt is banned. Confession and absolution as part of a weekly service? Gone. The chief of all penitential prayers, the Lord's Prayer? No way. The Law of God...it must not be mentioned!

Well, that is not completely true. The Law of God certainly is mentioned in the Church nowadays, but only as a standard to live up to, not as a mirror of our lives which shows clearly that we are not, nor can we, live up to such a standard. Put in another way, the Law of God is not used to make anyone feel guilty, simply to give Christians a goal to attain.

"No, no, no!" you may be thinking at this point. "The Law is still necessary for someone to realize that they need Christ!"

Okay, but then what is next for the new Christian? "Well, I'm not too sure here, but it would seem that now that I am a Christian, I really don't need to worry about the 10 Commandments anymore. I mean, does the Law of God still apply to Christians who have been redeemed by Christ? Have not Christians been freed from the Law? Cannot Christians simply live the way they want to live, free from the fear of doing something that our heavenly Father would not like? Can't Christians live lives of joy, regardless of how they live from day to day?"

These questions were posed to Martin Luther toward the end of his life. What follows is his thinking on these questions.

[1] As quoted in *Day by Day We Magnify Thee: Daily Readings for the Church Year Selected from the Writings of Martin Luther*, compiled and translated by Margarete Steiner and Percy Scott (Philadelphia: Fortress Press, 1989), p. 193.

[2] Mark 1:15.

1

WHAT IS REPENTANCE?

Repentance is the *sadness* we experience after committing a specific sin as well as the *resolution* we then make not to sin in such a way again. Such sadness is the feeling or awareness in our heart or conscience that we have disobeyed the Law of God (the 10 Commandments: Exodus 20; Deuteronomy 6). Many people hear the Law, but because they do not feel the effect or power of the Law in their hearts, experience no sadness, and so are not truly repentant.

The first part of repentance (sadness) is caused solely by the Law of God. The second part of repentance (the good resolve not to sin in such a way again) cannot be caused by the Law. The person who becomes terrified when he considers his sin cannot by his own strength alone resolve to do better.

In fact, the exact opposite occurs. When a person is overpowered by his sin and is ashamed of what he has done, he begins to mistrust God and actually to hate Him. Such mistrust and hate of God the Bible calls literally a descent into hell (Psalm 88).

In order to change this situation, the promise of Christ (the Gospel) must be added to the Law. It is the Gospel which lays the terrified conscience to rest and rights it once again so that a person can resolve to do better.

Repentance which is a result of the Law alone is only partial repentance, the beginning of repentance, or a repentance which is not complete. Such a repentance is not complete repentance for it does not include a resolve to do better. Such a repentance is just like the repentance of Cain (Genesis 4:13), Saul (1 Samuel 26:21; 31:4), Judas (Matthew 27:4-5) and all those who doubt and despair of the mercy of God.

Repentance which is a result of the Law alone is only partial repentance

Such a definition of repentance (*regret* for sin along with the resolution to do better) has been taught for centuries but with little understanding. Since the individual parts of the definition (sin, regret, and the resolve to do better) were not understood, repentance itself could not be taught.

What was taught instead was that such regret was really a product of a free will which possessed the ability to hate sin or not to hate sin whenever it wanted. In reality, regret is the sorrow or torment experienced by the conscience (whether it wants to or not!) when properly addressed or confronted by the Law.

Regret is the torment experienced by the conscience when confronted by the Law

In the past it was also taught that sin was simply an improper action against man-made institutions. Seldom were sins addressed that were committed against the moral law (the 10 Commandments). As far as original sin is concerned, it was taught that after baptism there should be no sin—especially a sin against any of the first three commandments.

The Law itself, described by Jeremiah (23:29) as God's rock-smashing hammer, crushes such an inaccurate teaching of repentance by enclosing all people in sin. According to such a faulty teaching, a good resolve not to sin is a thought self-chosen by human strength to avoid sin from a given point forward. But according to the Gospel, such good resolve is a movement of the heart awakened by the Holy Spirit.

A good resolve not to sin in a certain way again is the determination to hate sin from that time onward out of love for God—even though sin in the flesh still fights hard against such a determination. Being versed only in the rules and theories of men, and not in the Word of God, those in the past who taught otherwise understood neither the Law nor the Gospel–and so could not teach rightly about repentance.

In contrast to such a futile teaching of desperation the Gospel teaches that repentance is not despair alone, but hope as well. Such hope is a hate of sin which flows from a love of God. This is truly a good resolve not to sin.

---

1. Which are the two parts of repentance?

2. What causes the first part, the sorrow, of repentance?

3. What causes the second part of repentance?

4. What happens when a person resolves to do better, solely on the basis of the Law?

5. Who, in the Bible, repented of their sins, but not completely?

6. Why is it a problem to think that repentance is a result of a free human will?

7. What or who moves a Christian to resolve to do better?

8. According to Luther, how does Christian hope relate to sin?

2

DO CHRISTIANS REALLY NEED THE LAW?

Nowadays there is a novel idea afoot! According to the promoters of this idea, the Law (that is, the 10 Commandments) should be completely removed from the Church. This is nothing else but deplorable and irreverent.

The entire Bible teaches that it is the Law which must initiate repentance. Logic as well as experience teaches us this. That is why Scripture says: "The wicked shall return to Sheol, all the nations that forget God" (Psalm 9:17); and: "Put them in fear, O Lord! Let the nations know that they are but men!"(v. 20); "Let them be put to shame and dismayed forever;...that they may know that you alone, whose name is the Lord, are the Most High over all the earth" (Psalm 83:17); and "The wicked are snared in the work of their own hands" (Psalm 9:16).

In that we are human beings, we encounter sin and death before we encounter righteousness and life. We do not sin and die because we are righteous and alive. Rather, in that we are by nature sinful and die because of Adam, we must be made righteous and alive by Christ. The doctrine of Adam (that is of sin and death) must be taught before that of Christ–whom Adam prefigures (1 Corinthians 15:47).

Sin and death are not exposed by a Word of grace and comfort, but only by the Law. Experience proves this as well. Adam was first rebuked as a breaker of the Law, and then restored through the promised descendant of the woman (Genesis 3:15). David also was first killed through the Law, when Nathan said to him: "You are the man!" He was then restored by the Gospel, when Nathan said: "You will not die" (2 Samuel 12:7,13). Paul was first struck down through the Law, and heard: "Saul, Saul, why are you persecuting Me?" Then he was made alive again through the Gospel: "Get up" (Acts 9:4, 6).

> **The doctrine of Adam must be taught before that of Christ–whom Adam prefigures**

And Christ Himself said (Mark 1:15): "Repent, and believe the Gospel, for the Kingdom of God has come among you!" And afterwards (Luke 24:46f): "The Christ must suffer etc. and allow preaching of repentance and the forgiveness of sins in His name."

The Spirit first rebukes the world because of sin (John 16:8) so that He can then teach faith in Christ, that is, the forgiveness of sins. Paul in Romans held to this way of teaching when he first taught that all people are sinners and then afterwards, that they must become righteous only through Jesus Christ (Romans 3:23, 28). Luke as well asserts in Acts that Paul taught both the Jews and the heathen that no one can become righteous, except through Christ alone (Acts 13:38).

---

1. What "novel idea" was being promoted in the Church of Luther's day?

2. Is that same idea being promoted today?

3. If so, in what way is such an idea being promoted?

4. According to the Word of God, what is it that must cause a person to begin to repent?

5. Do we, as Christians, still encounter sin and death?

6. Do we encounter sin and death before or after righteousness and life?

7. Luther gives three examples of people in the Bible who were first exposed to sin and death, and then righteousness and life. Name them:

8. Did Christ preach about sin and death, or only about righteousness and life?

9. Which person of the Trinity convicts the world of sin?

10. Why does He do that?

3

NOT TO MAKE US RIGHT BEFORE GOD!

The Law cannot make us righteous before God. It is completely unuseful and unfulfillable. The Law will become a poison and a pestilence to him who believes that he will become righteous before God by fulfilling the Law.

If someone examines the doctrine of justification, not enough can be said against the powerlessness of the Law, and against the destructiveness of a trust in the Law. The Law was not given to make righteous, or alive, or help in some way to justify man (Galatians 3:21). On the contrary, the Law exposes sin and creates wrath

(Romans 3:20; 4:15), that is, the Law creates guilt in the conscience.

Death is not imposed upon us to give us life. Sin is not inborn within us to make us sinless. The Law was not given to us so that by keeping it we would become righteous. The Law is not able to give righteousness or life.

In short, as far as the east is from the west, so far should the Law be separated from the Gospel. One simply should not teach, say, or think about a person's righteousness before God with anything but the Word of grace, which was made known to us in Christ.

This does not mean, however, that the Law has become obsolete. This does not mean that the Law should not be part of the preaching of the Church. In fact, because of the grace made known to us in Christ, the teaching of the Law is even *more* necessary.

> **The teaching of the Law is even more necessary because of the grace made known to us in Christ**

Why? It must be made known that the fulfilling of the Law is not only *not* necessary for our justification, but simply impossible! Only by the preaching of the Law will the self-centered person who is confident in his own abilities be taught that he cannot become righteous by the Law.

Sin and death must first and foremost be revealed to such a person. These must be revealed to him, not because they are necessary for righteousness and life, but in order that he acknowledges his unrighteousness and his condemnation - and is humbled.

If sin remains unacknowledged, a person imagines himself guiltless (as was the case among the Greeks and thereafter among the Pelagians[1]). If death remains unacknowledged, a person will think that this life is all that there is and that no future life exists.

[1] Pelagians were followers of the British monk Pelagius (late 4th, early 5th century), who denied the doctrine of original sin and taught that Christians had a free will not only in earthly matters, but in spiritual matters as well.

---

1. If a person tries to become righteous before God by fulfilling the Law, why will such a person's view of the Law change?

2. As far as the doctrine of justification is concerned, does the Law have any power?

3. For what purpose was the Law given?

4. Why is the preaching of the Law necessary?

5. What does the Law do for the "self-centered person who is confident in his own abilities" and strength?

6. Why must sin and death be revealed to such a person?

7. What happens if sin remains unacknowledged?

4

BUT TO EXPOSE SIN, WRATH AND DEATH

The Law alone teaches both sin and death. The Law is therefore extremely useful and necessary.

The work of the Law–both in the Old and New Testament–is to expose sin, wrath and death. The exposing of sin is nothing else (and *can* be nothing else) than the Law, or the proper work and working of the Law.

The expressions *Law, exposing of sin,* and *revelation of wrath* are synonymous, just as the terms *man* and *reasonable creature* are synonymous. To discard the Law and still maintain some sort of revelation of wrath is just as if you would deny that Peter was a human being, and yet claim he was a reasonable creature. It would be just as wise to discard the Law and yet assert that sin must be forgiven.

The Writings of the Holy Spirit maintain that sin remains dead without the Law, and without the Law there is no breaking of the Law (Romans 4:15). Sin, therefore, cannot exist or be acknowledged without the Law–either the Law written in our hearts or the Law in the Bible.

It follows then that since there is no sin, there is no Christ who redeems from sin. It is, after all, Christ who said: "The healthy do not need a physician" (Matthew 9:12).

Christ did not appear to abolish the Law but to fulfill it (Matthew 5:17). If there is no Law which we should fulfill, Christ appeared for no purpose. And because the Law demands our obedience to God, anyone who would discard the Law would effectively put an end to our obedience to God.

> **If there is no Law which we should fulfill, Christ appeared for no purpose**

It should therefore be clear that the devil alone uses such an assertion to teach us about sin, repentance and Christ. By doing so, however, he takes Christ, repentance, sin and the entire Scriptures away from us.

Taking these things away from us, the devil thus takes away from us the author of Scripture, God Himself, and intends to establish the most destructive security, contempt for God, unpunished wantonness, and an eternal unrepentedness greater than that of Epicurus[1] himself. Such an intent is proven by the claim people make today that "*all the Law is used for is to condemn people to hell! Certainly the job of rebuking sin via the Law is not a work of the Holy Spirit!*"

Yet these same people would still continue to talk about the forgiveness of sins. But how can there be sin at all, when sin does not have the power to condemn a person to hell? Obviously then, there must be some sort of sin that does not damn! Perhaps this special kind of sin also makes a person holy without Christ!

> **A sin that does not damn is better than both righteousness and life itself**

You see, when sin does not damn, we have not been redeemed by Christ from a damnable sin. If we have not been redeemed by Christ from a damnable sin, we have not escaped the wrath of God.

A sin that does not damn is a sin which is better than both righteousness and life itself. For what could be holier than to have sins which do not damn, which are, in reality, not sins at all? If the Law is abolished, we must be redeemed by such undamnable sins, and must be holy, and must not have Christ be our Mediator before God.

It is also false to assert that the Law rebukes sin without the Holy Spirit. After all the Law is written with the finger of God (Exodus 31:18). All truth, where it exists, is from the Holy Spirit. To abolish the Law is therefore to abolish the truth of God.

It is simply nonsense to abolish the Law because its work is to rebuke sin to damnation. The power of sin is the Law, as St. Paul says (1 Corinthians 15:56), and sin itself is the sting of death. Otherwise, let us eat and drink and being led by such a teacher sing: "Away with anything which prepares us for tomorrow!" For after the Law (which is the power of sin) is discarded, it must be that death and hell are destroyed. Such destruction occurs not through the blood of the Son of God, who perfectly obeyed and fulfilled the Law, but in that we simply deny that there is some sort of Law of God that must be fulfilled!

> **All truth is from the Holy Spirit; to abolish the Law is therefore to abolish the truth of God**

All such teaching nowadays about sin, repentance, Christ and the forgiveness of sin is simply nonsense and a lie entirely worthy of the devil. For as the Law was before Christ, it freely accuses us. Under Christ, however, the Law is fulfilled through the Spirit and silenced through the forgiveness of sins.

The Law after Christ will remain fulfilled in the life to come. At that time the creature will have become new (just as the Law now demands that it be!)

For this reason the Law will not be discarded, but will remain, so that it must either be fulfilled by the damned, or become fulfilled by the holy. What is taught today, however, is that the Law remained in effect only for a time, and ceased under Christ, as did circumcision.

[1]Epicurus (342?-270 B. C.) was a Greek philosopher who taught that the only good thing in life was pleasure. In that pleasure was the only good thing in life, pleasure should be the ultimate arbiter of what is moral.

---

1. What alone teaches both sin and death?

2. Would it be possible to discard the Law of God and still speak about His wrath?

3. Can sin exist without the Law?

4. If sin does not exist, do we need Christ?

5. How does discarding the Law take from us sin, repentance, and ultimately, Jesus Christ Himself?

6. If a sin does not have the power to damn a person to hell, is it still a sin?

7. Can the Law rebuke sin without the Holy Spirit?

8. Why is it that sin is tied so closely to the Law and damnation?

9. How is the Law "fulfilled through the Spirit?"

10. How will the Law be fulfilled in the life to come?

5

CHRISTIAN REPENTANCE IS CONTINUAL

The repentance of Roman Catholicism, Islam, Judaism, unbelievers and hypocrites is all the same. All express sorrow for a few real sins, and then make satisfaction for them.

To other unknown sins, or original sin itself, however, they remain oblivious. Their repentance is therefore partial, and temporary, only in view of a few sins, and over a few small periods of time in their lives. But such must be the view of repentance by anyone who does not understand that the entire human nature through original sin is dreadfully damaged and corrupted.

The repentance of those who believe in Christ does not focus in upon actual sins alone, but is continual, the whole life long, until death. It is the duty of Christians to hate and abhor the lingering disease of sin in the human nature until they die.

Christ says rightly to all who believe in Him "Repent" (Matthew 4:17). Christ wants the entire life of those who believe in Him to be one of repentance, for sin remains in our flesh as long as we live and fights against the Spirit, which opposes it (Romans 7:23).

All works after justification, therefore, are nothing else then a continual repentance—or a good resolution against sin. To do such works is to do nothing else than to drive out the sin which through the Law is exposed and through Christ is forgiven.

> **All works after justification, therefore, are nothing else than a continual repentance**

The doing of such works is similar to the task given the children of Israel after the land of Canaan had been conquered. Their victory assured, they were to drive out the remaining Jebusites who still dwelt in the land (Deuteronomy 7:1). Of course, it wasn't any easier driving the remaining Jebusites out of the land than it had been initially to enter it! In a similar fashion, it is not much easier–through continual repentance–to drive out the sin that remains within us than it was initially to become an enemy of sin.

This is the reason why the holy and just (when God so works upon them with the Law) are often sad in heart and lament their sin. By rights they should rejoice in the Lord, for their sins have been forgiven, and they remain in grace (Romans 5:1; 8:1). And yet they cry out pitiably, mentioning no real sins, and pray simply for the grace of God, just as we read in the Psalms.

---

1. How is the repentance of Roman Catholicism, Islam, Judaism, and even atheism similar?

2. How does true Christian repentance differ?

3. As long as we live, what fights against the Holy Spirit, which opposes it?

4. How are all works, after justification, nothing else but continual repentance?

5. How is repentance similar to the driving out of the Jebusites from the land of Canaan by the Israelites?

6. Why is it that Christians, who should rejoice, are often sad in heart?

6

THE LORD'S PRAYER IS A PRAYER OF REPENTANCE

The Lord's Prayer, which was taught by the Lord Himself to His holy and faithful disciples (Matthew 6:9-13), is a part of repentance. It is also something taught by Christ in which a great deal of the Law remains. For whoever prays the Lord's Prayer rightly, confesses with his own mouth, that he sins against the Law, and for that, he is sorry.

Whoever prays that God's name should be holy confesses that God's name is not yet completely holy. Whoever prays that the kingdom of God should come confesses that he still, in part, remains in the kingdom of the devil–to which God's kingdom is opposed. Whoever prays that God's will be done confesses that he, in greater part, has been disobedient to the will of God–and for that he is sorry.

In that the Law of God teaches that the name of God should be hallowed, whoever prays such a thing confesses that he has not fulfilled this Law. And whoever abhors what from the kingdom of the devil still remains within him, he at the same time, confesses that he has not fulfilled the Law–especially the first three commandments. And he who prays that God's will should occur within him confesses that he has not been obedient to the will of God.

This prayer must be prayed by the entire Church until the end of the world. This prayer must be prayed by each individual saint until death. For the entire Church is holy, and acknowledges that it has sin, and must repent without ceasing.

The Lord's Prayer itself teaches, therefore that before a Christian is declared righteous, when he is declared righteous, and while he is considered to be righteous, the Law should remain. It also teaches that repentance must be initiated by the Law. For whoever asks for something simply confesses that he does not have that thing for which he asks, and waits for that thing to be given to him. It is the Law which shows us what we do not have, and still necessarily must have.

> **Whoever asks for something confesses that he does not have it and waits for it to be given to him**

It should be no surprise then that whoever wants to get rid of the Law must also get rid of the Lord's Prayer. Come to think of it, they must get rid of the greatest part of the preaching of our Lord Jesus Christ Himself. For He Himself (Matthew 5:17ff) not only discussed the Law of Moses, but fully interpreted it, and taught that it should not be dissolved.

And in that He taught the Pharisees about the most important and greatest commandment of the Law, He sanctioned the Law, and said: "Do this and you will live" (Luke 10:28). The Lord chastised, reproached, threatened, and frightened throughout the Gospels and so practiced the same office of the Law. Those who teach that the Law must be done away with are therefore simply ashamed to teach and to do what the Lord Himself taught and did.

> **Those who do not teach the Law are ashamed to teach and do what the Lord himself taught and did**

But let's suppose, for the point of argument, that sin could be exposed by something else besides the Law (which is nonetheless impossible!). Should we therefore get rid of the Law because it does the same thing that is done by something else, that is, it exposes sin?

Along these same lines, if the Law could be done away with in its *written* form, who would want to utterly destroy the *living* Law, which is written in the heart, and is in opposition to us, and is simply the same as the Law of Moses (Colossians 2:14)?

1. Why is the Lord's Prayer called the Lord's Prayer?

2. How is the Lord's Prayer part of repentance?

3. For centuries, the Lord's Prayer has been prayed right before the Words of Institution and the distribution of the Lord's Supper. Why would that be?

4. In that we pray for many things in the Lord's Prayer, what are we actually confessing about those things by praying for them?

5. Even though the Church is holy, does sin still remain within it?

6. What is it that shows a Christian what he does not have, and yet still must have?

7. Why must those who want to get rid of the Law, also get rid of the prayer which Jesus taught his disciples?

8. Did Jesus teach that the Law should be dissolved, or fulfilled?

9. Even if something else besides the Law could expose sin, should we get rid of the Law?

7

THE FORGIVENESS OF SIN IS CERTAIN

There hasn't been a more destructive teaching against repentance in the Church (with the exception of the Sadducees and the Epicureans) as that of Roman Catholicism. In that it never permitted the forgiveness of sin to be certain, it took away complete and true repentance.

It taught that a person must be uncertain as to whether or not he stood before God in grace with his sins forgiven. Such certainty was instead to be found in the value of a person's repentance, confession, satisfaction and service in purgatory. It never declared, however, *when* the end of repentance, confession, satisfaction and purgatory would be.

But who would repent of anything for any length of time if there were no certainty as to whether or not sins were retained or forgiven? Of course it was not the unrepentant and confident people who were taught such a thing, but the terrified, who had begun to repent in such a way, but eventually would be moved, out of desperation, to cease to repent at all.

> **Who would repent of anything if there were no certainty as to whether or not sins were forgiven?**

To anyone who would repent in such a way Christ would be useless. Why? Such a person would always be in doubt as to whether or not Christ had died for his particular sins!

Such doubt, which leads to perpetual unrepentance, is more dangerous than even the unrepentance of the confident. The unrepentance of the confident is disdain for God. In contrast, perpetual unrepentance is blasphemy against the Holy Spirit.

Therefore one must protect himself against such a doctrine of repentance as much as one protects himself from hell and the devil himself.

1. Why is it that if a Christian is not certain that His sins are forgiven, complete and true repentance is not possible?

2. Would a person repent of anything, if he were not sure that his sins had been forgiven?

3. Why would Christ be useless to such a person?

4. What is, ultimately, perpetual unrepentance?

8

Repentance, However, is Vital!

A Christian must simply guard himself against those who would not allow any kind of repentance to remain in the Church. For they who say that one should not teach the Law teach in reality that there should be no repentance whatsoever.

The argument that "What is not necessary for justification, neither beginning, nor middle, nor end, should not be taught" is worthless. To begin with, if you would ask what these bombastic words 'beginning', 'middle' and 'end' mean you will find that they themselves do not understand them.

It is as if you would conclude: "There is nothing necessary for justification in the fact that man is dead in sin–neither in beginning, nor middle, nor end–therefore one should not teach such a thing." Or "To honor parents, to live chastely, not to murder, not to commit adultery, and not to steal is not necessary for salvation, therefore one should not teach such things." Or "That man is obligated to serve within the government of state and home, is not necessary for salvation, therefore any Law which addresses such a thing should be abolished."

> *It simply does not follow that since the Law is not necessary for salvation it should be abolished*

If the meaning of such an assertion is that anything not necessary for justification should not be taught, what then is new? It simply does not follow, that since the Law is not necessary for salvation it should be abolished– or at least cease to be taught.

In support of such an idea, the experience of Paul and Barnabas–through whose service the heathen were justified without the Law (Acts 13)–is falsely applied. For Paul proved that all men are sinners (which is the work of the Law) even as he taught that all men must be made righteous through Christ alone (Acts 13:38).

You see, whoever wants to be justified is still a sinner and will only be convinced of that fact through the Law. Throughout the writings of Paul, the phrase "without the Law" should therefore be understood as Augustine[1] rightly understood it, "without the *assistance* of the Law."

For the Law does not *assist* us in fulfilling it, but instead, *demands* that we fulfill it.

In fact, the Law demands this from us to such an extent that it will not allow one vain word to remain unprosecuted—as Christ Himself affirmed. The Lord also noted that "not an iota, not a dot, will pass from the Law, until all is accomplished" (Matthew 5:18). In short, if Christ is not set against this strong admonisher the Law, payment for guilt must be made to the last penny (Matthew 5:26).

Grace and the forgiveness of sins do not make people safe before sin, death and the Law to the extent that sin, death and the Law no longer exist. On the contrary, grace and forgiveness make us far more industrious and careful to overcome sin, death, and the Law daily through Christ, the One Who makes us holy.

The Law of God is not part of our lives merely because *we* want it to be, but instead, it is part of our lives *whether or not* we want it to be. The Law of God was part of our lives before we were justified, is in the beginning, middle, and end of justification, and is part of our lives even after we are justified. The Law is there because it had to be taught, acknowledged, and reign from the beginning of sin, which Adam started, until it would be fulfilled through Christ, the Victor.

Faith in Christ alone justifies (Romans 3:28). He alone fulfills the Law. He alone does good works without the Law. He alone

After justification good works freely follow without the help or the coercion of the Law

receives the forgiveness of sins, and does good works through love by His own free will. It is true that after justification good works freely follow without the Law, that is, without the help or the coercion of the Law.

In summary, the Law is of no use nor necessary for justification. Neither is it of use nor necessary for any sort of good work–much less for holiness. The opposite, in fact, is true: Justification, good works and holiness are necessary for the fulfilling of the Law. For Christ is come "to seek and save the lost" (Luke 19:10), and "to restore all things" (Acts 3:21).

The Law, therefore, was not *abolished* through Christ. Instead, the Law was *established* once again in order that Adam would be as he once was and even better still.

[1] Augustine of Hippo (354-430).

---

1. Why is it that if the Church stops teaching the Law, it must also stop practicing repentance?

2. In that the Law is not part of justification, does that mean it is not part of the Christian life? Why or why not?

3. Does the Law assist us in fulfilling the Law, or merely demand that we fulfil it?

4. Are there any sins that a Christian commits, even sins of the slightest nature, for which no compensation to God is required?

5. Since a Christian enjoys the grace of God and the forgiveness of sins, do sin, death and the Law cease to exist?

6. Is the Law of God part of life merely because we want it to be? Do we have a choice as to whether or not it should be?

7. What alone justifies us before God?

8. Who alone does good works from His own free will?

9. After justification, do good works flow from a Christian without the coercion of the Law?

10. Was the Law, through Christ, abolished or established?

9

THE LAW RULES OVER MAN AS LONG AS HE LIVES

"The Law is binding on a person only as long as he lives" (Romans 7:1). This means that a person will be free from the Law only when he dies. Consequently, if a man wants to be free from the Law, it is necessary that he dies.

In that the Law rules over man as long as he lives, sin also rules over man as long as he lives. Therefore, if man wants to be free from sin, he must die. For "the Law is the power of sin, but sin is the sting of death" (1 Corinthians 15:56).

These three, the Law, sin and death, are inseparable.

Therefore, insofar as death remains in man, sin and the Law also remain.

Apart from Christ we receive the Law, that is, the letter, which is not yet fulfilled, and yet necessarily must be fulfilled by us. *In* Christ the Law is certainly fulfilled, sin exterminated, and death destroyed.

That means that if we, through faith in Christ, are crucified and die, in such a way is the Law truly fulfilled, sin truly exterminated, and death truly destroyed also among us. As long as we do not die in such a way, we are still not in Christ, but instead are outside of Christ, and therefore under the Law, sin and death.

The doctrine itself demonstrates–and experience proves–that people who are justified continue to die with as much frequency as people who are not justified. In that the justified still experience death, they must still be under the Law and sin.

> **In that the justified still experience death, they must still be under the Law**

Those who want to remove the Law from the Church are totally inexperienced people and deceivers of souls. For such a thing is not only foolish and godless, but also completely impossible. For if you want to take away the Law, you must at the same time take away sin and death. For death and sin are present through the Law, as Paul says: "The Law kills" (2 Corinthians 3:6); and "The Law is the power of sin" (1 Corinthians 15:56).

In that you yourself can see that justified Christians continue to die daily, it is simply foolishness to think that Christians should be without the Law. For if there were no Law, there would be neither sin nor death.

It must therefore be demonstrated that the righteous are either completely without sin and death, are now no longer living in the flesh, or have been taken out of the world. If such a thing could be demonstrated then we could do away with the Law and cease to teach it. Since experience demonstrates the exact opposite, however, any person who would want to remove the Law from the Church should simply be ashamed of himself.

---

1. How long does the Law rule over man?

2. What must happen to a man, to be freed from the Law?

3. How are sin, death, and the Law related?

4. How then is the Law fulfilled in Christians? Apart from Christ or in Christ?

5. Do Christians die with as much frequency as non-Christians?

6. What must be demonstrated before Christians can do away with the Law and cease to teach it?

10

THE LAW RULES OVER NON-CHRISTIANS AS WELL

Even more shameless still is the assertion that the Law should not be preached to a non-Christian. If the justified and holy must keep their sins and death constantly exposed by the Law—even though the Law is not given to them—how much more must the Law be presented to the Godless and evil, to which the Law is actually and truly given?

When it comes to the point where it is taught that the Church comes into being and Christians are pious without the Law, we have sunk into utter madness. At that point, we truly would not know what we were saying or doing.

To assert such a thing would be to think that all believers have been removed from the world. Such an idea would be simply fantasy. After all, in this world the two are mixed together: The justified who live still in the flesh, and the evil. As the Law was given to the heathen not to be rejected but to create awareness of sin, death and the wrath of God, so is the Law given to the holy, as far as they have not yet died, and still live in the flesh.

In the resurrected Christ there is no sin, no death, and no Law to which He was subjugated in life. But the same Christ is not yet fully resurrected in those who believe in Him. He begins within them, as firstlings, to raise them from the dead.

> **As far as Christ is arisen within us, so far are we without the Law, sin and death**

But in non-Christians, who are intermingled in the Church with the Christians, and whose number is greater than that of the Christians, Christ is still dead. He is not within them. Such people are solely under the Law, and must through the Law—yes, where it is possible—be terrified with bodily thunderbolts.

As far as Christ is arisen within us, so far are we without the Law, sin and death. As far as He, however, is not yet arisen within us, so far are we under the Law, sin and death.

For this reason the Law—as well as the Gospel—must be preached without discrimination both to the

Christian and the non-Christian. It must be preached to the non-Christian so that he is frightened that his sins are made known to death and the unavoidable wrath of God–and thereby is humbled. The Law must be preached to the Christian so that he is reminded to crucify his flesh with its lusts and desires and never to become secure (Galatians 5:24). For security takes away faith and the fear of God, and makes the state of the person to whom such a thing occurs far worse than it was before he became a Christian (2 Peter 2:20).

---

1. Should the Law be preached to someone who is not a Christian? Why or why not?

2. Why is the Law given to the non-Christian?

3. Why is the Law given to the Christian?

4. According to Luther, is Christ fully resurrected in those who believe in Him? Why or why not?

5. What about non-Christians? Is Christ resurrected within them?

6. What is the relationship between the 'riseness' of Christ within us and the Law, sin and death?

7. Why would security actually *take away* faith and the fear of God?

11

IN CHRISTIANS THE LAW REMAINS UNFULFILLED

Those in the Church who would do away with the Law of God suppose that through Christ sin is done away with essentially, substantially, and legally. Such people do not understand that sin is done away with *only in that God does not reckon it to them* (Psalm 32:2) and out of mercy forgives their sin. For only *relatively*, out of grace, not essentially, nor substantially, is sin suspended, the Law done away with, and death destroyed.

This happens according to the will of Christ in this life "until we all attain to the unity of the faith and of the knowledge of the Son of God, to mature manhood, to the measure of the stature of the fullness of Christ" (Ephesians 4:13). Christ was made a sacrament and an example for us. This wonderful thought is that of Augustine, who wrote: "Christ with his death according to the flesh, became one with us who were condemned in both body and soul, in order to restore us." But Augustine never implied by writing this–nor have we who read his writings therefore concluded–that we should do away with the Law.

This has been deduced, however, by those who would do away with the Law. Such a thought, therefore, is original to them and of their own making.

The Holy Scriptures show us four ways to preach and to bring people to holiness. These four ways are taken from four works of God: God terrifies with threats, comforts with promises, admonishes with sufferings, and beckons with kindnesses.

But when these four ways are taught, they do not do away with the Law, but instead, strengthen the Law. "The goodness of God leads you to repentance" (Romans 2:4), that is, so you acknowledge that the Law is the power of sin (1 Corinthians 15:56). In that now the Law frightens and kills, it does so because it refers man to himself, or in other words, drives man to knowledge of himself.

> **In that now the Law frightens and kills, it does so to drive man to knowledge of himself**

These folks who would do away with the Law,

however, act in such a way, that through the sacrament and example of Christ they take away Christ Himself. For if the Law would be taken away, no one would know what Christ is or what He has done.

> **Without the teaching of the Law, Christ himself cannot be maintained**

Without the Law no one would know that Christ has fulfilled the Law for us. If I want to recognize the fulfilling of the Law, that is, Christ, necessarily I must know what the Law is and how it is fulfilled.

According to such people the Law cannot be taught. When one teaches the Law, he must teach that the Law is not fulfilled in us, and that we are therefore guilty of sin and death.

If the Law would be taught we would all learn that we are guilty of the Law and are children of wrath. The Godless would learn that they are guilty according to the flesh and spirit, or in other words, completely and entirely. Christians, however, would learn through the Law that they are guilty and children of wrath as far as they still are in the flesh and live.

For this reason the teaching of the Law is still necessary in the Church and must be maintained. Without the teaching of the Law, Christ Himself cannot be maintained. For what would you think of Christ if the Law, which He has fulfilled, is done away with and you do not know what He has fulfilled? Ultimately the Law is fulfilled in Christ in such a way that you cannot teach the Law *unless you also teach that the Law is not fulfilled in us.*

To get rid of the Law, and allow sin and death to remain is nothing else than to cover up the pestilence of sin and death in people to their destruction. When death and sin are done away with–as Christ has done (2 Timothy 1:10; Romans 8:3)–then the Law can happily be done away with, that is, the Law can finally be established (Romans 3:31).

---

1. If we would do away with the Law of God, what would we be saying about sin?

2. How is sin done away with in the Christian: Substantially, legally or relatively?

3. How was Christ made a sacrament and example for us?

4. What are the four ways, taught by the Word of God, to preach and bring people to holiness?

5. How does the Law frighten and kill?

6. Is Christ truly knowable without the Law?

7. What does the Law teach the Godless?

8. What does the Law teach Christians?

9. When can the Church finally cease to teach the Law?

12

THE LAW MUST CONDEMN

The conclusion of Saint Paul, that "where there is no Law, there is no trespass" (Romans 4:5), is not only spiritually, but also physically and naturally true. It is also true to say: Where there is no sin, there is neither judgement nor forgiveness of sin. Also true is the assertion: Where there is neither judgement nor forgiveness, there is also no wrath or grace.

The same is also true: Where there is no wrath or grace, there is neither divine or human government. The same is also true: Where there is neither divine or human government, there is neither God nor man. The same is also true: Where there is neither God nor man, there is nothing, perhaps, except the devil.

Therefore it must be that those who would rid the Church of the Law are either devils themselves, or siblings of the devil. It doesn't matter that they preach and teach a great deal about God, about Christ, about grace and the Law.

It is neither novel nor unique that the name of God is used improperly–as the devil himself often has done. The confession of those who would rid the Church of the Law is just like when the devil cries out to Christ "You are the Son of the Living God" (Luke 4:34; 8:28). It is also like the oath of every false prophet, "As true as the Lord lives!" as Isaiah and Jeremiah show.

> **Whoever says that one should not teach the Law which damns simply denies the work of the Law**

Whoever says that one should not teach the Law which damns, simply denies the work of the Law. And if such a person would actually teach something from the Law, he would be teaching the veil of Moses, not his clear and actual face (2 Corinthians 3:13). In other words, he would be teaching the Law as understood solely by the flesh.

The Law which does not damn is made-up and constructed in much the same way as the mythical figures of the Pegasus and mermaids. Even worldly or natural Law is nothing if it does not frighten and condemn the trespasser (Romans 13:1,5; 1 Peter 2:13ff). Therefore it is rightly said: "From bad morals come good Laws."

What those who would eliminate the Law from the Church say about God, about Christ, about faith, the Law, grace, and other things is said in much the same way as a parrot says "Hello," that is, it is said without understanding. It is simply impossible that one can learn good theology or right living from such preachers.

Therefore one should run away from their teaching as the most harmful teaching of libertines, who give permission to all sorts of infamous deeds. For "they do not serve Christ, but their own stomachs" (Romans 16:18) and seek, as people without sense, to be pleasing to others, so that in return, they can be honored by them.

---

1. Why is it that if there is no Law, there is no trespass?

2. Can a person preach the Law of God improperly? How?

3. What does Luther mean, when he compares those who teach the Law of God improperly in the Church, to the demons which cried out "You are the Son of the Living God"?

4. What is the difference between the veil of Moses and his actual face?

5. What does it mean to teach "the law as understood by the flesh"?

6. How is the Law which does not damn like the Pegasus, the flying horse of Greek mythology?

7. How is a teacher in the Church who would not teach the Law like a parrot who can say "Hello!"?

8. How do false teachers in the Church serve not Christ, but their stomachs?

Afterword

"Why can't Christian worship be simply, totally, and completely joyful?" This question, raised by a parishioner, drove me to delve into the question of the penitential nature of traditional Christian worship. It was, after all, the penitential aspect of Christian worship, which if anything, could be considered the culprit in the situation. Who, after all, can be joyful when confronted by sin for which he is responsible?

Why then the penitential aspect of Christian worship? Why is it, I asked myself, that for centuries, Christian worship has begun with the confession of sins, continued in the *Kyrie* with pleas for the Lord to have mercy on the Christian, proceeded with the ultimate prayer of repentance, the Lord's Prayer, and finally, just before the reception of the Lord's Supper, included the *Agnus Dei*, that is, the plea that the Lamb of God, Christ, have mercy? Why not simply remove these four elements from Christian worship?

The answer to this question, and the others posed above, I found in the Antinomian theses of Martin Luther. Written in the years 1537, 1538 and 1540, these sets of theses for 6 separate disputations addressed the appropriate use of the Law of God among Christians, and thus, in Christian worship. What moved Luther to write these sets of theses were the assertions of a Wittenberg theologian by the name of Johannes Sneider, (1492-1566) a.k.a, Johannes Agricola.

Agricola, a long time colleague of Luther, had begun to preach and teach that the Law should no longer be taught in the Church. Agricola believed, apparently, that a person became aware of sin not from his or her awareness of the Law of God, but from his or her awareness–and complete acceptance–of the Gospel, i.e. Jesus Christ. According to Agricola, a person was sinful not because he had broken one or all of the commandments, but because he had rejected Christ. This being the case, the Law had no place in the Church. Only Christ, only the Gospel, should be preached by Christian pastors.

According to Johann Georg Walch (1693-1775), the translator of the original theses into the German text from which this translation was made, a sermon constructed along these theological lines would first and foremost inform parishioners of the grace and mercy of God in Christ Jesus. What would then follow would be the penetrating question as to whether or not the parishioners truly believed in the grace and mercy of God through poverty, sorrow, sickness, and the fear of death. If through self examination, the person found that they were guilty of unbelief, what they were then encouraged to do was to call upon God in prayer.[1] (Nowadays we hear this approach to the Gospel most frequently when this question is posed: "Have you made Jesus Lord of your life? If you have not, please pray with me now...")

For the good of his students then, and for the Church (he thought), Luther wrote these theses which take Agricola's understanding of the Law and flesh it out by asking the simple question: If what Agricola is teaching is true, what does it ultimately mean for the person and work of Jesus Christ? Luther's answer was that it negated them both.

The six sets of theses are divided in this book in the following fashion:

Disputation # 1	Dec 1537	Chapters 1-2
Disputation # 2	Jan 12th, 1538	Chapters 3-4
Disputation # 3	1538	Chapters 5-6
Disputation # 4	1538	Chapters 7-8
Disputation # 5	Sept 13th, 1538	Chapters 9-11
Disputation # 6	Sept 10th, 1540	Chapter 12

Where, then, did I find these theses? Prof. Roland Ziegler, of Concordia Theological Seminary in Ft. Wayne, Indiana should be mentioned here as the ultimate source, for he is the one who in his current lectures on systematic theology has been delving into these disputations and other works of Luther that address the usage of the Law in the Church. His musings on these texts have, through his students, gone well beyond the city limits of Ft. Wayne.

Article VI of the Formula of Concord (1577), *The Third Use Of Law*, is a result of discussions raised by Agricola's theology and Luther's response in these theses and other works of the period. In his *Historical Introductions to the Book of Concord* (St. Louis: Concordia

Publishing House, 1921, pp. 161-172), F. Bente sketched an outline of the issues at hand and therewith included many of the theses here published.

The theses published here were not gleaned from Bente's *Historical Introductions*, however, but were translated into English from the German translation of the Latin text by Walch, published in volume 20 (columns 1628-1649) of his 24 volume edition of Luther's works. These were first printed in the years 1740-1752, and again in St. Louis in the years 1880-1910. My source, as was Bente's (presumably), was the St. Louis edition (see footnote above). Of other English translations of the Antinomian theses of Martin Luther I am unaware.

The chapter headings as well as the study questions were added for clarity. Bible citations were standardized–when possible–using the new English Standard Version (Wheaton: Crossway Bibles, 2001).

Here I must thank Scott Krieger for reformatting the entire text and, in general, seeing the work through to its publication. Without his tireless efforts, it simply would not have been possible. Gene Berner and Cornelia Murphy read through early drafts of this work and were extremely helpful in their questioning of muddled translations.

For the shortcomings of this work, I freely take responsibility. Surely others could have faired better with bringing a 16th century academic treatise into 21st century light. Yet, what is truly important is that this work, in whatever form, is once again read and embraced by the

Christian Church. If this edition, then, helps in some way to cause this to occur, its flaws, I hope, will be graciously overlooked.

Paul Strawn, Spring Lake Park, Minnesota
October, 2004

[1] In the words of Walch: "1. Die Art und Weise, diese Lehre unter das Volk zu bringen, soll diese sein: 1. Dem Volke soll Gottes Gnade und Barmherzigkeit in Christo aufs allerfüsseste gepredigt werden. Das ist die Major (propositio). 2. Darauf soll das Volk aufgefordert werden, sich zu erforschen, ob es das auch völlig glaube in Armuth, Krankheit, Schande, Todesschrecken und anderem Unglück. Das ist die Minor, die hauptsache, wo die nicht folgt, da ist noch kein Evangelium gepredigt, sondern, daß Christus ein rechter Moses sei. "Auf den Minorem folgt: conclusio in hunc modum": 3. "Wer sich nun schuldig weiß, der rufe Gott an"..." In "31. D. Martin Luthers Widerlegung der falschen und verführischen Lehre der Antinomer wider das Gesetz, in 6 Disputationenen verfasst," Dr. Martin Luthers Sämmtliche Schriften, edited by J. G. Walch, Vol. 20 (St. Louis: Lutherischer Concordia-Verlag, 1890), Col. 1624, ftnt. 2.

Biblical References

Genesis		Jeremiah	
3:15	24	*23:29*	21
4:13	20	Lamentations	
Exodus		*3:22-33*	15
20	19	Zechariah	
31:18	33	*9:9*	10
Deuteronomy		Matthew	
6	19	*4:17*	38
7:1	38	*5:17*	32, 43
1 Samuel		*5:18*	51
26:21	20	*5:26*	51
31:4	20	*6:9-13*	41
2 Samuel		*9:12*	32
12:7	8, 24	*27:4-5*	20
12:13	24	Mark	
Psalms		*1:15*	12, 17, 24
9:16	24	Luke	
9:17	23	*4:34*	68
9:20	23	*8:28*	68
32:2	64	*10:20*	10
51:10-12	11	*10:28*	43
83:17	24	*19:10*	52
88	20	*24:46f*	24

John
- *16:8* — 8, 25
- *16:16-22* — 15

Acts
- *3:21* — 52
- *9:4,6* — 24
- *13* — 50
- *13:38* — 25, 50

Romans
- *2:4* — 64
- *3:20* — 9, 28
- *3:23* — 25
- *3:28* — 25, 51
- *3:31* — 66
- *4:5* — 67
- *4:15* — 28, 32
- *5:1* — 39
- *7* — 15
- *7:1* — 55
- *7:7-8* — 8
- *7:23* — 38
- *8:1* — 39
- *8:3* — 66
- *13:1* — 68
- *13:5* — 68
- *16:18* — 69

1 Corinthians
- *15:47* — 24
- *15:56* — 34, 55, 56, 64

2 Corinthians
- *3:6* — 56
- *3:13* — 68

Galatians
- *3:21* — 27
- *5:22-23* — 9
- *5:24* — 61

Ephesians
- *4:13* — 64

Philippians
- *4:4* — 10

Colossians
- *2:14* — 43

2 Timothy
- *1:10* — 66

1 Peter
- *2:13ff* — 68

2 Peter
- *2:20* — 61

1 John
- *3:1-3* — 15

Lutheran Press

is a non-profit corporation established to publish and promote the theology of Martin Luther. Although many of Luther's works are already available to the general public, their publication as part of collected works editions has prevented them from being widely disseminated. Of special interest to Lutheran Press are the smaller topical works of Luther that continue to address the Christian Church today, but nonetheless, remain effectively unknown. The mission of Lutheran Press is to make such works available on the internet free of charge and by mail at a minimal cost, with proceeds used to publish additional works.

To learn more about Lutheran Press or to order any of our books please contact us at:

Lutheran Press, Inc.
1728 132nd Lane NE
Minneapolis, MN 55449

Lutheran Press
Minneapolis

www.lutheranpress.com

How To Live A Christian Life

Adapted From
Martin Luther's
On Christian Freedom

In this short work, Martin Luther answers the question of how to live a Christian life by harmonizing two seemingly contradictory statements by the Apostle Paul, and in doing so clearly and simply explains the basic aspects of the Christian life.

To order *How To Live A Christian Life* please contact us by mail or online at:

Lutheran Press, Inc.
1728 132nd Lane NE
Minneapolis, MN 55449

www.lutheranpress.com